THROUGH LIFE'S WINDOW

poetry Pt today

THROUGH LIFE'S WINDOW

Edited by Suzy Walton

First published in Great Britain in 2000 by Poetry
Today, an imprint of
Penhaligon Page Ltd, Remus House, Coltsfoot Drive,
Woodston, Peterborough. PE2 9JX

A Catalogue record for this book is available from the
British Library

ISBN 1 86226 660 3

Typesetting and layout, Penhaligon Page Ltd, England.
Printed and bound by Forward Press Ltd, England

Foreword

Through Life's Window is a compilation of poetry, featuring some of our finest poets. This book gives an insight into the essence of modern living and deals with the reality of life today. We think we have created an anthology with a universal appeal.

There are many technical aspects to the writing of poetry and *Through Life's Window* contains free verse and examples of more structured work from a wealth of talented poets.

Poetry is a coat of many colours. Today's poets write in a limitless array of styles: traditional rhyming poetry is as alive and kicking today as modern free verse. Language ranges from easily accessible to intricate and elusive.

Poems have a lot to offer in our fast-paced 'instant' world. Reading poems gives us an opportunity to sit back and explore ourselves and the world around us.

Contents

My Thoughts Of You

The sky was blue, the sun was gold,
And all seemed like a dream untold,
I sat there with my head afloat
As onward came a tiny boat!
It settled near a willow tree
Which lapped the waters right by me!
A duck began to cross the grass
And I just watched it quickly pass,
My heart leapt up with sheer delight
To witness such a lovely sight!
I stood for nearly one whole hour,
At all the plants which were in flower!
An angel coming down to land
Beside the sea, upon the sand,
Could not have formed a lovelier view
Than when I fell in love with you!

S Howells

The Soul's Compassion

Take pittance on the poor and needed for they shall seek love,
Take pittance on the careless and good for they shall seek the truth,
Take pittance on the devil and the wicked for they shall seek evil,
Take pittance on the soul for you shall seek love,

With every delicate whisper your voice tickles my heart, breaking the
                                    harshness in this cold world,
With every soft kiss your lips weaken my bones,
Soft and gentle hearts treat me with desirability,
So touching and with tender warmth,

Take pittance on the lonely and the likeable for they shall seek
                                    companionship,
Take pittance on the lost and strayed for they shall seek a direction,
Take pittance on the young and old for they shall seek youth,
Take pittance on the soul for you shall seek sympathy,

With every neat step your feet soothe my grave,
Breaking the truth of an inevitable death,
With every slender movement your body changes the brave to the
                                    afraid,
Soft and gentle hearts change my ability,
So sensitive and with tender grace,

Take pittance on the innocent and blamed for they shall seek justice,
Take pittance on the shy and the coy for they shall seek affection,
Take pittance on the bewitched and the believed for they shall seek
                                    fascism,
Take pittance on the soul for you shall seek empathy,

With every memorable episode your face heals my wounds,
Breaking the ice in this painful fog,
With every shining sparkle your eyes melt my life star bound to the
                                    sky,
Soft and gentle hearts rotate with prevailing flexibility,
So sensuous and with tender passion,

Take pittance on the bold and brash for they shall seek patience,
Take pittance on the distressed and the heroic for they shall seek
                                                                    stamina,
Take pittance on the king and the queen for they shall seek fortune,
Take pittance on the soul for you shall seek compassion.

Gaz Thompson

John

Hold my hands and you will know
I am always here for you,
Hold my hands and feel the strength
There is enough for two,
Hold my hands and feel the love
From a sister to a brother,
Hold my hands and we will ride
This roller coaster together.

I wish that I could take your pain
And wash it away like the falling rain,
I wish that I could take your fears
And turn them into happy years,
But all I can do is to offer you
My hands for you to hold,
Please hold them tight and don't let go
For I need you more than you will ever know.

Mary Neill

The Old Blacksmith Shop

An interesting place was the old blacksmith shop
The blacksmith would hammer away on irons red hot
Sometimes I pump the bellows at the forge till I did tire
The blacksmith beating irons into shape after heating in the fire

The ring of the hammer on the anvil you would often hear
A leather apron to protect his clothes he would wear
The hammer on red hot iron would send sparks flying
I couldn't lift the hammer it was no good me trying

I've watched farmers bringing horses to be shod many a time
The shoes were tried on while still hot the horses didn't mind
Then the shoes were dipped in water before they were nailed on
Horses used on roads would go lame without shoes on

The wheelwright would bring his wagon and cart wheels round
For iron rims to be fitted so the wheels were tightly bound
But now we have tractors and trailers with metal wheels and rubber
tyres
Gone is the sight of the blacksmith working with red hot irons in the
fire

The smell of hot irons on horses hoof all is quiet and not a sound
The blacksmith is a dying breed few if any can be found
But the blacksmith was a familiar figure in my childhood days
Since then the world has changed in so many ways

Harry Skinn

A Special Place

A special place I found,
when I was only three,
at the end of a garden path,
a meadow with a tree.

I toddled up the path with ease,
and found to my great pleasure,
in the meadow, lambs to tease,
and a shady Oak to treasure.

Sad the day when we moved away,
to another home, so far away.
Exploring further I was thrilled to see,
a meadow with a Walnut tree.

What games we played upon that tree,
one day a ship upon the sea.
It could be anything we wanted,
even a ghost ship that was haunted.

Then wandering nearby, one day,
in another meadow not far away,
a truly wonderful sight to see,
a fully-fruited Mulberry tree.

A place to visit again and again,
our fingers with Mulberry juice we stain.
Then we run to the pond,
where a tree overlooks
and sit in the sun reading our books.

My children now play by a pond, with some trees,
and they have found there are moorhens to tease.
When all had grown up, and left us alone,
we searched for a perfect place of our own.

We found our meadow with a great Oak tree,
we knew we'd be happy, just you and me.
But later still there is only me,
in the house in the meadow, with the great Oak tree.

P Bryan

Epitaph

Lie not I here, for I am far away,
On swallow's wing I fly the ripening grain,
In rainbow curves I praise the raining day,
By flowing stream the gliding fish betray,
But not to Earth my shadow falls again
Or in the breathless soil is sombre lain.

Lie not I here, from here my Soul has flown
To river banks and margins of the lake,
And in the celandine is newly grown
Beside the furrowed fields as newly sown
The growing green of summer bank and brake
Betrays Eternity has come awake.

Lie not I here, nor would I wish to be,
For I am with the falcon or the teal,
Or with the otter, swimming warily,
Or on the snowy hill where roe deer see
The imprint of the fox abroad to steal
A sleeping hare the shadows long reveal.

Lie not I here, from here I am long gone,
My Life though run is not in earth engraved,
For I have flown like Autumn leaves undone,
Now ever in the Water, Air and Sun
To live an endless life no trials braved,
Free as the Peregrine, nor less enslaved;
Lie not I here.

John Peaston

Rusty

Rusty follows the shepherd
In rain, hail or snow
Everyone is a friend
Faithful collie is he
No cats allowed in his territory
Barks jumps runs
Cats in terror flee
Wags his tail with delight
When Ginger the cat spits in fury
Then seeks refuge up a tree.

Rusty now contented
Curls up and has a sleep
Shepherd calls Rusty
Time to collect the stray sheep
Runs bounding with delight at his master's feet.
Day's work now ended
Farm work complete
Rusty and Ginger
Scurry to the hay shed
Ginger the cat sleeps undisturbed
At Rusty's tired feet.

F Gibson

Go Back

Oh let's go back to Christmas
To when Jesus Christ was born
Oh let's go back to Christmas
To that stable all forlorn
Yes let's go back to Christmas
And remember why He came
If we go back to Christmas
We will bow our head in shame.

We've made it so commercial
Just a time for food and drink
Oh let's go back to Christmas
Just let us stop and think
Yes let's go back to Christmas
Then we'll celebrate His Birth
Yes let's go back to Christmas
We'll bring Joy and Peace to Earth.

Terry Wray

Last Resort . . .

You take my heart away from me
You take the very best of me
You took my love and ran through town . . . spreading dirty rumours
round
I guess I was the sad old 'clown' when the circus came to town
Once I was as high up as the Trapeze
Picking stars . . . and swinging on trees
Drinking cheap champagne beneath the moon
It couldn't have ended all that soon . . . Honey on a silver teaspoon
I take you to be my lawful wedded sweetener
You can make everything complete now
I melt under the heat of your gaze . . . you stir me . . .
. . . And I dissolve completely . . . another problem . . . now to solve
The sticky bit at the bottom of the 'mug' . . .
As we lie entwined on a threadbare rug . . . a bit of sangria . . . left in
the jug
I guess I was the liquid refreshment . . . at the time . . a good
investment . . .
As we signed . . . the pre-nuptial agreement . . . love . . . not a
business arrangement
You'll kill me in this Kangaroo court . . . at this manic seaside resort
We listened to House music . . . danced in the Garage . . . we both
thought . . .
. . . It was pretty 'savage' we danced till we dropped . . . but I never
liked House
music . . . well . . . not a lot . . . I thought it was a load of crap . . .
so . . .
Let's sort out the sleeping arrangements . . . now we're single . . .
Justify our derangements . . . So send me a postcard . . . when you get
there. . .
. . . Next year but I will definitely wish I was not 'here'
I am just a commodity when there is no beer . . . and someone will be
crying
But they won't be my tears . . . I guess it was the last *resort* . . .

Sally Wyatt

Old Age

I'm really past my sell-by date.
My future's looking bleak.
My eyesight's not as good as yours;
And all my limbs are weak.

I tend to say, 'When I was young . . .'
It drives my daughter potty.
'Don't you worry about aged mum,'
Says she, 'She's really rather dotty.'

She smoothes my brow and tends the fire,
It's all so rather grim.
She pets and strokes and fusses me,
As if I am quite dim.

'Tomorrow is your birthday, mum,'
She tells me far too brightly,
'And I must say that for your age,
You're really rather sprightly!'

My daughter brings me tea in bed,
Which makes me feel quite naughty.
'It's for aged mum,' she says to friends;
Although I'm only forty!

Rowena Gregory

The Hills

In the far distance they stand,
Like sentinels upon the land;
Their summits pointing to the sky,
As if lifting our gaze on high.

Their colours have to be seen,
Varying from dull grey to vivid green:
It depends upon the changing light
What shades impinge upon our sight.

To climb those hills is such a task;
Too much for some of us to ask
Ourselves, although we can but try;
We scramble up with many a weary sigh.

The stony ground beneath our feet
Makes climbing these hills such a feat;
We look upward to what lies ahead,
To look down fills us with dizzy dread.

The experts climb up the mountain's face,
However slow and hazardous their pace;
They cling to the rock with hands and feet,
Skilled to face whatever they may meet.

And when at last they reach the peak,
They hardly have enough breath to speak;
Lying down upon the ground to rest,
They know that they have survived the test.

But those of us who cannot climb that way,
Still discover that the hills have much to say;
They tell us that if we lift our wondering eyes,
We will see the God who made the hills and the sky.

Kenneth E Jinks

Woodland Walk

Trees stand tall and proud,
Green leaves adorn the branches,
Sheltering creatures,
Large and small,

A breeze stirs the trees,
Some stray leaves flutter to the ground,
Grass and flowers intermingle,
A dizzying spectacle of colour,

A sense of calm envelopes the wood,
Dawn has broken,
Woodland creatures emerge,
Searching for food,
Light streams through the canopy of trees,

It's high noon,
Humans have arrived,
To witness its tranquillity and stillness,
Some people are silent during the walk in the woods,
Frightened to disturb nature in its glory,

We are always too busy to stop and look,
Wait for a second, breathe the air,
Bask in the splendour,
You never know what you may experience.

Enjoy your time in this enchanted wood,
It holds many secrets,
For the right person to see,
Fairies, Goblins, Pixies and more,
Go on, do it, explore.

Emma Scrivens

Blue Innocence

That man-made path you have taken,
better company than man you now keep.
On broken wings you have risen, this dying world forsaken;
few will know and even fewer weep.

Shadows come and go, the sun rises;
the world keeps turning and the manrats race.
You were nought; the irrelevant and defenceless Man despises,
what he has judged and sentenced to oblivion with words alone he
will replace.

You knew no words, asked no favours, could not fight nor sanctuary
find.
The shadows came and stayed, the sun set on a fading wing.
No epitaph, no splendid past remembered by a better world for Man
is blind;
recall and smile a rye smile for me in the days when darkness is king.

Our world is dying; when Man is no more I may be free.
For I am Man, the guilt is mine, yet my despair and regrets are true.
So if we meet and if you see a friend, reach out and call to me.
For, Blue Innocence, I reach out and call to you.

*(The Great Blue, a butterfly, now extinct in Britain due to destruction
of habitat.)*

Dave Shea

Dreamcycling!

One day we cycled to Widecombe,
Across the moor for miles and miles.
At last we'd arrived and we did come,
To a friendly welcome and Devonian smiles.

We each drank some cider and ate a pasty,
And down yer in Deb'n nothing's hasty.
We said our goodbyes to those lovely folk,
Which seemed like hours with their jovial talk.

Then we got on our bikes and wobbled away,
And we somehow felt heavier that day.
We didn't really mind as we're not watching the clock,
And leisurely travelled to old Tavistock.

Where we partook of dinner and later to beds,
And what pleasant dreams entered our heads.
We set out next morning on our way to South Devon,
And the weather was glorious we thought it was heaven.

That beautiful county like paradise did seem,
But on opening our eyes 'twas only a dream.
We found ourselves back in London,
We were working at our jobs,
No time to tell what really went on,
A stark antithesis, Rat Race and mobs.

Nigel T Membury

Whiskers Galore
(A True Cats Tale)

We have this band of local cats, and sometimes the odd stray,
Each will come a'calling, all hours of night and day,
They loaf around our gardens, with no desire to roam
The trouble is, they eat us, out of house and home.

There's 'Hunter' and 'Big Jessie', then 'Annie', who's so shy,
Poor 'Oliver's' not quite all there, since losing his left eye,
At night, with just his right one, what a tricky puzzle knowing,
It's hard to tell, by Moonlight, if he's coming or he's going.

Their role in life is obvious, these cats were, 'Born to scoff',
To the 'Ginger Tom', minus one ear, we gave the name 'Van Gogh',
'Rizzi's' years the oldest, but 'By Heck!' she eats and drinks,
She's been around so long, they say, 'She modelled for the Sphinx'.

'Albert' is a Siamese, though in truth, 'Albert's' a she,
With a cunning knack of visiting, at breakfast, lunch and tea,
'Scrapper' is the 'Wild One', no one cared enough to tame,
Then comes 'Doppel-ganger', she and my cat, look the same.

'Flipper' was abandoned, when neighbours came to find her,
Just like my cat 'Marmite', who's another, left-behinder,
Once there was this kitten, who came in with 'Marmite',
This lively tabby rascal, charged around all night.

Our Motley-crew's so laid-back, they would not chase a mouse,
But at the slightest hint of rain, they stampede for the house,
Finally there's 'Bossgags', I can't think of any more,
But, 'Lord knows, what's' in waiting, when I open the back door.

If there's one consolation with all these cats we're feeding,
It's a blessing they're all, 'Neutered', and have no hope of breeding,
Time to end this hairy tale, and feed our hungry brood,
Then, once again, go shopping, for a ton of Moggie-food.

Kevin D Clapson

Our Generous God

Put not our trust in 'nobles'
Nor in the sons of men,
But look to God who changes not
And will do all He can
To give you wisdom from above
To meet the fears you have
Apply His word in daily life
And then you will know 'love'.
His qualities are clearly seen
If you will look around
At all the wonders in the world
They truly do abound.
The dewdrops are God's diamonds
More precious than the stone,
The smallest insect, it's his drink
He sips on his way home.
That shaft of sunlight through the trees,
God's fingers, point the way
To lighten forest dense within
On glorious autumn day.
For soon enough chill winter comes
With snow to cover ground
A blanket warm for seeds below
Each year by us are found.
Our constant God sends rain to fall
On good and bad the same,
Acknowledge this and call on Him,
Thus glorying His name.

Laura Duncan

The Jailbird

The jailbird lives within a nest
    That's built of stone and steel
He lives alone, he has no mates
    No-one knows how sad he feels

The jailbird sings a long sad song
    You can hear him sing at night
It's a song that all the jailbirds know
    A song of loneliness, a song of fright

The jailbird often has to fight
    If he is to stay alive
He also has to live by rules
    If not, he can't survive

He sits alone from day to day
    Through sunshine and through rain
He is not allowed to leave the nest
    He only has himself to blame

The jailbird tries to get away
    To be free and have some fun
Bu this jailer will not let him go
    Until his time is done

The jailbird is a funny name
    I guess you may ask why
Well the jailbird, has no wings
    So the jailbird cannot fly

    Peter James Hartley

The Way Of Laughter

I love to laugh and have a giggle
It makes me feel quite good
Although my body is racked with pain
My brain's not made of wood.

I thank the Lord I have my senses
Without them I would die
To see the funniest side of things
Is something that I try

I am sure laughter is a tonic
To all who will join in
A few good jokes can set a pattern
And cause a great big grin

The best thing of all to make us laugh
Are odd things that we say
Words that are twisted or mispronounced
Can start us on our way

This does no harm to anybody
To laugh at these mistakes
Some in writing are much funnier
The laughter gives us aches

Sometimes laughter is infectious
And makes us all impart
And when we look at one another
We all just fall apart

Edith Buckeridge

Small Piece

One small piece of a man
Change universe big plan
Scientists crack DNA code
Set universe better mood

Tomorrow computer brain
Help body to take big strain
Short route to one heaven
Midnight hour's left eleven

Long know some no human
Bunched to gather a reunion
How long before make all like
Mass produce, wings on bike

High time a piece was made
Replacing diamond a spade
Practical experience do count
With this can remove mount

But a piece take away *'daft'*
Replace practical super craft
Open show world its mistake
All aim to make universe Great.

J J Flint

Addiction

The whispers left inside the Womb
And some of that was me.
The shadows that infest a Room
And tried to strangle me
The soil, the grass, the rocks, the
Leaves, the moss that paints a
Tree
A squirrel that floats swiftly by
That's part of you and me.

And more and more and more
And more and give me more
And more
'I'll give you peace,' it said to me
Just give me more and more
A lifted latch, a bag that's snatched
A broken windowpane.
A penny saved's a penny earned
'I won't come back again.'

The salted taste of tears at night
A promise meant to keep.
You give me joy, I give you pain
You cry yourself to sleep.
But deeper in my pain I sink
In torment my soul cries,
'The pit is deep there's no way out
I'm trapped by my own lies.'

G A Brooks

22

Nature Is Free

The beauties of nature are one of the free things of
life. We are generally able to enjoy them without finance.

However, nothing in life is totally free!

We can enjoy a forest but we have an obligation to prevent
despoliation.

Trees give us lumber, clear water and bind the soil to prevent erosion.

We must protect all nature.

Nola B Small

Name Me The Birds . . .

Name me the birds, which give us so much joy,
Whose nests I robbed, when I was just a boy.
Half the fun was finding each one's site
And climbing up to get a closer view.
We were not told to do so was not right;
We took the eggs if there were more than two.
We built up our collections so we might
Swap, like stamp collectors do.

Each egg was pierced and carefully blown,
(To remove the bits that might have flown)
Lovingly polished and displayed,
A beautiful talking-point they made,
Their colours gave us so much joy,
When I was just a thoughtless boy!

Patrick Davies

Eclipse

Seconds
Pass
Where the moon
Defeats the sun
Turning day
Into night
Only
Swift
As
A Moment
Until the
Next celestial event
As the sun
Resumes
Its authority
Over day and night
Once more.

Anthony John Ward

Twilight Hour

As I wait till darkness falls
making shadows on the walls
In the evening light I am at home
Sitting with the dogs I love
lovingly they kiss my face
Then the peaceful solitude
all the outside world exclude
Then my thoughts come back to me again
and the moon
Like a spirit gliding through my room
Part awake and part asleep
dreaming long forgotten dreams
Then the present runs into the past
playing games within my mind
Now and then become entwined
like the roses as they die
Love was one great long goodbye
Then it all comes back to me again
and the moon
Like a spirit gliding through my room
I shut my eyes and the nightime images go by
and the moon
Like a spirit gliding through my room . . .

Jean Tennent Mitchell

Lifelong Friend

Who is this girl so old and sad
Limping along with a thorn in her pad?
Was she ever someone's pet
Who could not afford to pay a vet?
Her fur is dirty and full of fleas,
She has paddled in mud up to her knees.
But underneath this sorry state
There is a dog who will be great.

Who is this lovely golden girl
Walking to heel by my side?
Is she the one who yesterday
Seemed to have lost her pride?
Indeed she is, at length restored
By a kind and skilful vet
With head held high and tail gently waving
She is now my much-loved pet.

She is my friend and I am hers
Though we both are old and grey.
We shall comfort each other without any words
Till we reach the end of life's day.

Joyce Stewart

Forgive Me

Will you ever 'forgive me'
For the things I've said and done
Didn't mean to hurt you so
Don't you know, you're still the only one
No one else will ever do
I could search my whole life through
And know, I'd never find, another you
For just a moments pleasure
I've lost the one that's dear to me
The love I treasured, is now no more
Than just a memory
Mistakes, I know, I've made a few
It's true, but haven't we all!
With temptation all around
Some are bound, to stumble and fall!
And I have paid that price
I've lost my paradise
Never more, to see
The love light in her eyes.

Karl Jakobsen

A Precious Pet

He fought so hard to stay with us.
He didn't want to go,
Although he was so very ill
He tried hard not to let it show.
Because, he knew,
If him and us had to part,
He would leave us with a broken heart.
We never could replace him
He was beyond compare.
A wonderful companion and
A friend who was always near.
In happy times and sad times
He made his presence known.
He is no longer with us now
But I know he is at rest.
Sox, you were our precious pet.
Yes you were the best.

Eileen Patricia Dunn

Just Another Hour

God gave me an extra hour
To prove myself to Him.
So I intend to make the most ~
I'm going down the gym.
My figure, it needs working on
But I never have the time,
So I'll cycle, jog and tread the boards
Until I'm seven stone nine.
And if I've any time to spare,
I'll dash to the beauty club,
To have my wrinkles smoothed away
With a Polyfilla rub.
But sixty minutes don't go far
And miracles can't wait,
I'm afraid I'll need another hour
Just to have an estimate.

Angela George

Seascapes

Sand moves in a surge of ferocity
Wind surges across an empty beach.
Sea rages where a red flag blows.
We sit becalmed in an end of pier cafe
while men in wet suits
surf the raging waves.
Later we walk through Alum Chine
wooded, mysterious in twilight,
full of bracken, blackberry bushes
rhododendrons and malevolence.

Next day the sea is still and blue
foam washes its ragged edges
golden light reflects on the surface
and men and dogs walk the promenade.
This perfect summer lasts but
a few hours.
As dark clouds loom,
we climb steep cliffs,
leaving below transient memories
footprints in sand,
destined for extinction,
erasure by choppy seas.

Rosemary Orr

Summer Song

My windows open to the earth
the breathing of the land brings fragrance to my mind
fills it with flowers and long since faded memories
of childhood, and barefoot play.

Amongst falling rose petals we danced
pink and white of bridal veil
absorbed in each other, happy laughing children.
Oh perfect everlasting summer day.

Jackie Draysey

The Wild Primrose of Cavan
(Dedicated to the warm welcome of the McIntyre family in Ireland)

The wild yellow little primrose stole my heart,
A symbol so delicate of a fresh new start,
Breaking through the sod to shine so prettily,
It worked so hard just to be set free,

To give a golden hue on a barren land,
To give a barren heart hope to stand,
To move ever forward on to new beginnings,
Without regret of the past that is Oh! So chilling.

The wild yellow Primrose of Cavan is so welcoming
It says to me, 'Never mind your troubles just come on in,'
To a warmth that shines just like the sun,
It costs you nothing, stand still life has just begun

To give a golden hue on a barren land,
To give a barren heart hope to stand,
To move ever forward on to new beginnings,
Without regret of the past that is Oh! So chilling.

So sit down and enjoy all that there is,
Smile at the yellow primrose and life is bliss,
So honest, so simple yet strong, without pretence,
A way to live in heart and spirit without the fence

That separates and divides a barren land,
That takes away hope then who can stand,
We must persevere like the primrose, make new beginnings,
Fill our hearts with the pure joy of living.

Lore McIntyre

Taking One Day At A Time

As the sun rises,
you are there, waiting
to expose your well-rounded form;
throw caution.
Thrust your peaks towards the warmth;
peaks now void of thick cover.
Showing each rivulet, each runnel.
You care not,
lying wide open, flaunting your ample curves,
valleys once filled with fruits of abundance,
forests, now thinned of cover
by the ravishes of time, abuse, and greed.
Then, the undulating curvatures of your plains,
deserts, changing your form daily
to tease and titillate.

Yet, you age with dignity,
holding up against the maltreatment
fostered by your selfish children.
The demands of seasons upon your flesh,
the curse of disease leaving its mark,
sometimes hidden from view, until it's too late.
In spite of it all,
you live life to the full,
taking one day at a time.

Holding no regrets
awaiting the next sunrise.

Jules A Riley

Four Girls

Take four girls in a flat
Some say it is a duty
Others a necessary evil
Two out to work two at home

Finders keepers, confess all
Only our Catholic convented out
Two found the missionary zeal
Other two still outside society

Take four girls a sixties pad
Fitzwilliam Avenue somewhere
When will they ever learn
The names of the streets in Belfast

S M Thompson

A Year Of Trees

Brown blackthorn buds turn white in leafless March,
   But change their white for green in April's day;
Pale green leaves, darkening as they larger grow,
   Stand black against the moon in nights of May.
Bright roses, in their first pride, scent the air,
   But tire and wilt as May turns into June;
Horse-chestnut spikes and cherry blossoms die
   And gardens lose their colour all too soon.
July's low branches host dark ivy leaves,
   Hydrangeas' petalled balls turn pink or blue;
In heat of August we seek shady groves,
   September welcomes rose trees decked anew.
October swells the fruit and crisps the nuts
   And vies with summer as it colours leaves
And paints them, week by week, still deeper hues,
   As each tree from its myriad twigs retrieves
The minerals which have fed it, helped its growth,
   Then seals its leaves with cork, until the gales
Of riotous bleak November scatter wide
   The food for next year's springtime growth, then hails
December, when deciduous trees can take
   Their time of rest to gather strength again.
Then children welcome prickly Christmas trees,
   And Christians bless God's gift of Christ to men.
The leafless trees, in January, stand
   And flaunt their naked beauty to the world

In woods and gardens till, so soft and light,
 The snow has fallen on each branch, and curled
Around each twig, and clings to shapes of trees
 And beautifies their nakedness, until
The next month's rain ~ damp February's boon ~
 Can thaw the snow and icicles, and fill
The streams and ponds and every garden well
 With water so that neither man nor beast
May suffer thirst, and trees can sip and quaff
 Last year's discarded minerals for a feast.

Mabel Helen Underwood

May 2000

Gardens wept in drizzling raindrops
yet looking luminously lush
verdant fields forty shades of green
a rich backdrop for saturated, scurrying
people, hurrying to shelter
with upturned umbrellas
frowning faces
looking for the sun.

What rich pastoral places!
New lakes lay undiscovered
appearing overnight and
reservoirs rose to over-brimmed banks
of fast-flowing rivers tumbling
turbulently towards fast-flowing rivers
streams swelled past
waterlogged gardens.

Clouds several shades of slate grey
shapes and sizes
merged mysteriously like a fairy-tale
Hailstones hammered like frozen peas
Like vanguards of war
umbrellas united 'gainst May rain
relentless, incessant
Blossom fell like pink snow

Luminously lush
A surging rushing gush
of drains forever dripping
overflowing like underground lakes
searching for survival
rain fell upwards,
underneath my feet
like a tiny tidal wave.

Rain falling in a veil of tears
Hailstones hammering like frozen peas
Get a life when the weather clears
And where are the birds, butterflies, bees?
And this is the wettest May for years.

Judy Studd

Since I Met You

Here I sit with you my love,
Here I sit with you.
Where all the fairies
be my love,
Where all the fairies be.
Hiding in, this pink blossom tree of life
The rainbow's high
but looks quite nice.
And as the rain starts to pour,
The wishing well, becomes full
And as I toss my coin,
Down to make a wish
I am wondering
What is left to wish for,
Since,
I met you.

Tracey Rose

Empty

I feel empty inside
Like all is lost never to return
The images I keep stored in my head
I wish I could burn

I still feel the pain of the day
Like I was there, no other way
I wish I would heal on the inside
Until then I just want to hide

I don't want anyone near
Only the one that I hold dear
The one that I wounded, has he died inside too?
The one I talk of, I care for, that one is you

I see children in the street wherever I go
It just reminds me ~ will the pain ever go?
Will I be able to face my nephew, my niece?
Will I be able to sleep at night?
Will I ever find peace?

Louise Hart

Pigeon

fallen bird!
Upon filthy wings
you bear away our plundered solitude
that martyrdom
of worn out cities

yet like a poet
unbroken . . .
you return
still seeking bread
even when language fails
detecting a blue vastness
non-perishable of human memory

so! Maintain
your scorned presence here
softened by clumsy hands
enabling you
to rob the ground of crumbs.

Jason Lebor

Columbia

I run across stone buildings that once was a street.
I stand staring at the cracks beneath my feet,
Five point six Earthquake took the city from beneath.
I stand in a doorway watching people in despair,
Crying for their loved ones that are no longer there.
Is there anyone who can help us in this time of need?
Only mother nature can say. What will be, will be.
A child sits on some rubble that once was someone's home,
looking for her mother to take her home.
Stretching out her arms to every passing stranger in tears and
                                                    despair.
Wanting to be picked up but no one seems to care.
I run towards her, lifting her into my arms,
telling her she'll be alright.
I walk though panic crowds pushing me left then right.

I hand her to a soldier, knowing she'll be alright.

Jane Treloar

The Window Of Life

The window of life begins,
From the day that we are born.
When our eyes are fully open,
Showing our surrounds, like
a fresh early summer dawn.
But like our season's changes,
the view through the window changes too.
From lovingness to anger,
all these things we view.
We see the greed around us
and may feel so insecure.
But look out through the window,
feel the gift of life for sure.

John Hickman

Arise And Awaken

The sun comes out, to brighten all the dark places,
The flowers arise, and show us their sweet faces.
The squirrels gather nuts, then play hide and seek,
The birds stretch their wings, and gradually take a peek.
The bees are busy making honey, the ants work hard all day,
The worm buries itself in mud, to keep the birds at bay.
The dog sees the cat, and chases it through the park,
The owl cuckoos and twit twoos after dark.
The bats come alive at night-time,
And us we go to bed at this time.

Maria Carmen Lee Costello

Simple Things

With the Eyes of a Child, look at the simple things,
Clouds of White sailing by, wait of what the Day will bring
See the Colours of the Rainbow,
How they shine, how they glow,
Watch a brown Leaf, drifting gently from a Tree
See how it floats, how it is free,
Hear the Birds singing and watch them fly
Lean back in your Chair, observe the World going by
Let your Face be caressed by a warm Summer's Breeze
Young People in Love, watch them laugh, how they tease
Run through a Garden, full of green Grass and Flowers
Feel soft Rain on your Face, enjoy Spring Showers
Swim through green, clear watered Lakes
Touch velvety Snow, see the delicate Flakes
Embrace somebody you love, and show that you care
Have someone Special, with whom, all this, you can share.

Ingrid Böckmann

Rainforest

If you go down to the woods today
you're in for a big surprise,
if you go down to the woods today
you'll never believe your eyes.
For ev'ry tree that ever there was
is crashing down for certain because,
today's the day
the woodcutters have their business.

Picnic time for animals,
are the animals
having a lovely time today
behind steel bars and unaware
the wipe-out of their habitat?
Too few glades and water pools,
it's concrete floors
and lots of prying eyes.
At six o'clock
their mummies and daddies
can't take them home to bed,
because their homes are not in the zoo.

Chris Antcliff

They Played With A 'Wee Tanner Ball'?

My old uncle said to me, 'Football' was played
In the fellows spare time you see,
And they played with a 'wee tanner ball'.
Their wages if any were small, but 'the game' was
The source of pride to one and all!
'Football hooligans' were an unknown breed
And when 'The game' was over the supporters of the
Other 'team' had a drink in the 'local' together yes indeed!
Nowadays says my uncle to me, it's just as plain as can be
Overpaid players and big business and such have killed
'The sport' that we loved so much.
And 'football' is no longer 'a game'.

Flora Divers

The Shipwreck

The roaring waves of restless rushing sea,
beat constantly as doom, a dread tattoo.
Upon the ship perpetually and on.

Staring over watery graves,
through portholes blackened by the night.
Upwards to the darkened sky,
a whining wind and waves so high, so high.
Then down to the murky depths,
strained eyes that only darkness see,
No horizon in the gloom.
Where sea and sky appear ~ to disappear.

A gasp, how cold, to feel the blood drain from your veins,
The sudden clutch of fear that grasps and tightens round your heart.

No hope, such chill, your shrivelling stomach, tightening with fear ~
A scream, A cry, A hoarse and pitiful moan,
O God, please help, you must not let me die.

Fatty R

Beirut

City beautiful in sunlit robe
And guarded by her watching, shifting seas
So sometime silver mingling, half real,
As interchanging, silent coves they probe.
The ancient city dreams towards Europe
Seeming in a slightly twilight mood.
Phoenician quinqueremes transmute to steel
As jewelled planes surmount the heliotrope.

See now, how in the clouds of olive mist

The city, tantalising, can't resist
To wear her evening dress of sparkling bronze.
A million teardrops sparkle in their throngs.

Towards the velvet midnight let us tread.
Towards the teardrops, softly let us tread.

Elizabeth Stephens

Vandalise

This vandalised church they made it cry out in shame
Thro' its smashed roof falls those tears of crying rain
There's hardboard that looks like a large wood shutter
There is a steady flow of rainwater rushing down its gutters

The beautiful manse garden is overcome with dandelion weeds
There's a broken bird table where the house martins did feed
They have chopped down its proud row of large yew trees
There's a discarded beehive a home for the vicar's honey bees

They took the lead that was a cover for its wounded head
There lies a smashed stone cross that bears its heroic dead
The old clock never worked its hands were locked in time
Nobody has ever heard its tick, it forgets how to chime

Then those heavy machines came and from it hangs a steel ball
You can hear its agonising screams of pain coming from its walls
This weeping church is now dying in anguish on its final day
Its heart now lies broken in a ditch of mud and clinging clay

In a quiet evening many said they have heard its haunting songs
Thro' the mist of yesteryear will echo with the church's tuneful dongs
Its once beautiful lawns have become a parking space for cars
Where the vestry once stood has now become a restaurant's noisy bar

Its peaceful cemetery has now become a coaches parking space
And every headstone they have been removed from its quiet place
Where vicar once stood has become a row of busy ugly shops
And the village hall there now stands a vandalised bus stop

J F Grainger

All My Lifetime

Over all my lifetime
There's nothing I've loved more
Than all those years
Of being a Mum
With children I adored
I watched them grow
From day to day
I've shared all they've achieved
Have kissed and cuddled
Loved and guided
Been proud
Oh! Yes indeed
And in those days of growing up
The days were never dull
As hectic as a roller coaster
All parents will have known
They were my dear and lovely days
The need was always there
Now they have grown
They show their love
Still share in many ways
Those early days were special
The best I've ever known
And love still fills up every room
Our house is still their home

Jeanette Gaffney

Why

Nobody knows the reason,
Why
We are born,
We live,
And then we die,
No one wants to die,
But die we must,
And return to the earth,
In a pile of dust
Men work hard, and women too,
Because that is the way it seems,
To buy a house, and build some dreams,
Some men work just to be greedy,
They never think about the needy,
But do we really know our worth,
To live in this place
Named planet earth,
Are all things really what they seem,
When we walk in fields,
Of pastures green

R Scott

Once Beautiful Earth

There was once a great love affair
between man and his spiritual earth,
a love so binding, it ran deeply,
it has now been besieged by his curse.
That which once clothed and fed him
has now been stabbed in the back,
dragging the earth by its hair
the love affair began to crack.

For generations over men have ploughed and sowed
the might of industry came crashing,
casting iron and concrete over ancient stone.
Progression he called it,
a future which is set to be bleak,
he has left his spiritual partner bleeding
raped nakedly and weak.

Green house gases from the masses
has left little room to breathe,
the sun is drying out the earth's soil
as poverty strikes starvation, deep.

That which was thought to be immortal
will be ground down and spread across the universe,
the memory of mortal men will be remembered,
for the death of this once beautiful earth.

C Leith

The Little Stream

By verdant hill and glen you come,
 Child of the waterfall;
A whisper in the quiet wood
 Where oak and elm stand tall.

You sing with thrush and nightingale,
 Your mystic, sweet refrain:
What do you care if skies be grey,
 Friend of the wind and rain!

You wind your way to secret haunts
 By bracken, moss and fern;
Perchance to meet a kindred stream ~
 But never to return!

The wild flowers on your sunny banks
 Delight the honeybee,
While birds in ecstasy of song
 Look down from every tree.

O little silver stream, wind on,
 A-sparkle in the sun,
Until you reach your destiny,
 Where deep dark waters run.

Patricia McGavock

Citizen 2000

Can't get on a bus, school kids
won't walk half a mile;
Stuck on a train, yet another
points failure;
Arrive for work later than usual,
half the staff rung in sick already;
Start to get things done ~ and
the system goes down;
Mad rush to meet management
deadline only to learn ~ yes,
extended again!
No relief, no lunch, long afternoon
and just about ready to make
the Home Run;
Soon, feet up and relax (I wish!)
but family strife, no easy life;
A long walk through streets
paved with History's gold,
feeling old ~ as youths shout names
about wrinklies who wear
designer frames;
Cyclist hogging the pavement
sends shoppers running for cover;
Resentment boils over, and
I stand my ground;
Cyclist takes a tumble, calls
a copper ~ who takes my details,
says I'll get a letter and rails
how people my age should
know better . . .

Peace at last on a quiet hill
as dusk settles on my city;
World without pity ~ but none
so beautiful;
Kite flier taking on a rough wind
with pride ~ symbol
of humanity's
better side

R N Taber

Fruits Of Summer

The early blossoming flower from which fruit will soon come
Whilst the sun may become hotter and the ground drier the fruit ~
the fruit
it's water-juice fresher and better
For as to some animal it will give ~ have its such as it would seem to
provide taken from it
Which whilst given freely is taken as a gift of such season
The tree or shrub apparently complicit in this and would prefer it this
way
As to some flower a bee would come tasting its nectar and take to
more flowers of the same
But this other flower would not welcome the murmur of bees
And shun them as if from their sting and not seek their use
But instead hearken animals as such would eat and taste their
sweetness
As from memory they are drawn in this season to what they want
And would make the cost of it as they would over-fill
As the fruit now is ripe and they would see it and seeing it eat
But yet the season would end and the flower or tree become bare or
disappear altogether
But they did not die and the tree on which or from which fruit was
taken
has provided from its own flower and laden
To those who have eaten its one particular fruit such as was for its
own.

C J Bayless

58

Nothing Visual

No peeking stars tonight I fear
Just a blanket on the sky
Perhaps another night say I
As I now close my eyes

Abigail E Jones

Life's Road

The road of life is never wide and straight,
it twists, turns, sharply bends
and goes back on itself, a figure eight.
On turnings off the road you may find friends
then lanes may lead to others, also pleasant,
until they meet your road again ~ a crescent.

The villages, through which it winds,
are quiet havens, drowsy and at peace.
The sprawling cities, which the road then finds,
are soiled with dirt and turmoil without cease.
The road goes on, but has it got an end?
There are no easy maps made for to show
if it just stops around the next sharp bend
or, potholed, makes your weary feet go slow.

You cannot stop, you go you know not where.
And stuffed inside your overladen pack,
your memories and other things are there
to tell you that there is no going back.
As long along the road of life you wend,
looking forward, looking toward
an unknown destination and an unknown end.

D G W Garde

Mum Loves You

M aking plans, is hard to do
U nderstanding . . . what you're going through
M aybe, if only, you could express.

L asting feelings, of loneliness.
O bviously, as time goes by
V arious thoughts, will make you cry.
E ndless memories, they can't take away,
S incerely yours, forever and a day

Y et her love, will last forever
O ften think of her, leave you never
U ndying love, just for you,

In your heart, you know it's true.

Denise Chapman

Spiritual Home

Huge black ape, eyes full of pain,
rocked from side to side.
Baby ape clung to her back,
caged, no place to hide.
Mother ape, heart throbbing,
dreamed of Africa.

Zoo keeper, disinterested,
threw in chopped up fruit.
Shuffled off with barrow,
to feed another brute.
Mother ape, heart sobbing,
dreamed of Africa.

Old man in a wheelchair,
was pushed towards the cage.
He'd lost the power of speech,
seethed in pent up rage.
Mutely staring at the ape,
knew she should be in Africa.

A look of recognition,
passed between the two.
Tacit understanding,
of wanting life anew.
He could see it in her eyes,
the need in her for Africa.

The man put out his hand,
palm flat against the mesh.
Gentle ape then touched him,
with leathery soft flesh.
They both could feel the heartbeat,
of her beloved Africa.

Joan Enefer

62

Bluebells

Maytime bluebells shyly peeping
In the hedgerow; jostling campion's pink
Shading to palest columbine.
Nature's colour chart,
Saxifrage to speedwell
Nettle stars to buttercups.
And cow parsley, tall, matching hawthorn boughs
Heavy with creamy may blossom.

Onwards to the bridle path
Heading through the trees.
Each coppiced clearing dotted
With wood anemones gently swaying;
White wind flowers bending to the swards
Of bright green grass. Smothered by bluebells
As far as the eye can see.

Paint with vision's palette
The blues and hues. Bright and clear, near
Shading towards deepest violet as distance
Marches and the canopy above lowers
Its cape of leaves and branches knitted
Into sheltering ceiling, just allowing
Showers of rain, refreshing
Bells of singing blue.

Jean Greenall

A Millennium Revelation

We are in a divided society where some cannot grasp the new
technology.
With a conception where almost a lifetime's teaching is incorporated
in a tiny chip ~ that's how it's going to be.
There has always been a distinction where the thirst for knowledge
and determination has left students over-tired.
Now much of the laborious study is eliminated and often to press a
key here and there is all that is required.
Some opinion was that the calculator would restrict use of the brain.
But it allows absorption of more knowledge and now the computer
supersedes again and again.
So much has happened in such a short time that many do not
understand it yet.
We do see even the youngest children quite at home with the Website
and the Internet.
Some will be unable to handle the complexities and that will always
be.
But there may be more dependency on mundane jobs to support the
super wizardry.
And so there will be a selection with a creation of opportunities that
were not there before.
Not forgetting that all progress originated in someone's dream and
imagination with basic reading and writing ~ it will be so for
evermore.

Reg Morris

Dune

The light winds coax the grains,
Around the dancing blades of grass,
That line the crest,
Where footprints rest,
In these ever so shifting sands.

Of dried out kelp and stick,
Of rope and ancient crate,
Strewn on the shore,
By winter storms,
Where the rolling surf did break.

They are streaming past the clouds,
The rays of a closing day,
Their golden lights,
Now shimmering bright,
In the ripples and the evening waves.

The young girl of the castles,
Watch her playing in the lee,
She pats the sand,
With gentle hands,
As her hair is blowing free.

Surrounded by her shells,
Her infant's thoughts so clear.
Her time runs slow,
Her memories grow,
She's a million miles from here.

There are seagulls on the wing,
The sentinels of the sky.
They circle high,
With haunting cries,
As another day passes by.

Stuart R Boyd

Disappointment

I sit and watch the hands of the clock,
Moving slowly towards the hour.
Only twenty more minutes to go
Before that knock on the door.
I wish I had prettier cups to set out,
But these will have to suffice,
I suppose the cups won't matter that much
So long as the tea is nice.
Oh dear I haven't dusted that shelf
But perhaps they will not see
After all they're not coming to examine my flat,
They said they would come and see *me*.
I very seldom see anyone
I can't go out any more
I seem to spend my life now
Hoping for a knock on my door
But today I know I'll hear that rat-tat-tat
Visitors coming to tea.
That cake looks a bit sad in the middle
But again ~ perhaps they will not see.
I sit and watch the hands of the clock
Moving swiftly past the hour.
I guess they just couldn't make it.
So it's tea ~ just for one ~ once more.

Irene Spencer

Quality Time

It's a wonderful spring day,
In the early part of May,
The sun is shining, and the world has come alive,
And we have gone out for a drive,
Everyone looks happy in the sun,
Enjoying themselves, and just having fun,
We are going to stop for lunch in a pub,
A nice Sunday roast, lovely grub.

After that, we will have a walk,
Quality time for us, time for ourselves, just to talk,
Then we will drive home slowly,
And arrive back just in time for tea,
We have travelled far and wide, you and me,
But on days like today, England is where we love to be.

Maureen Arnold

The God Tree

For the great oak to grow
The roots search and toil
Before branches spread out
A seed seeks out soil

The young sapling grows
Into a mature strong tree
Seasons pass through time
Still it remains for all to see

Lightning flashes with thunder
Storms howl and blow
The tree survives the ravages
Of wind rain and snow

Following the path of creation
Our lives should always be
A testament to survival
Like the struggle of the tree

For roots that hold firm
Plant faithfully in the Lord
The food for existence
Is in the covenant of His Word

As a sapling alone
Without protection or care
We would wither and fade
Into dust mist and air

This is the law of nature
Clear and plain to see
The tree needs the roots
The roots need the tree

Measureless in expanse
Withstanding a storm
The tree is a structure
That is timeless in form

Our Lord and Saviour guides us
His wisdom is everywhere
The God Tree ~ His precious symbol
Shatters doubt conquers fear.

Cynthia Antoinette Roomes

Joy In The Countryside

We have found walks with others a joy
There is so much to inspire friendship
When with others in the countryside
The joy of observing the wildlife
As we progress along a pathway.
During the twentieth century paths
Have for our joy been well developed
In many areas of our land.
We owe much to the National Trust
Such areas allow much freedom
For all the generations to come.

John Roberts

Broken Hearts

in the midst of a giant green theatre feel the
ageless trees bow down to greet the newborn sun
smell the fresh sap rising from the bark
hear the birds sing in the evening light
no broken hearts

flying high the parrots flash by
blazing a trail through the depths of the forest;
tall trees reach for the sky
sheltering life below their thick shrouded boughs
no broken hearts

man enters with giant spades
digging up this sacred ground
massive blades mow down antique woods
clearing the forest for houses for mankind
so many broken hearts

flatten the woods we want more books
we don't care if the globe is dying
we don't care if the earth overheats
who cares about the wonder of nature
what does it matter if the rainforests die
every one a broken heart

the blue of the sky covered with thick grey smoke
smelling the flowers no longer sublime
listen to the birds croak in the smog
broken-hearted they struggle along

hear the hearts breaking of people who care
people who love the beauty of nature
people who love this wonderful world
every one a broken heart

Fiona Higgins

Sand

Lying on the warm sand,
My body so close to the Earth
That tiny particles cling
To my skin
And reflect the sun's
Pearly brilliance
As I allow a steady flow
Of white granules
To trickle through
My fingers . . .

Earth's treasures and
The beauty of nature
Sparkling before my eyes
Has remained in my memory
And been a source of solace
To me at times of sadness
Or during cold winters ~
Far from my childhood home.

Earth's inspiration in this form
Has stayed with me
Throughout my life
And this scene holds
A sacred place of warmth,
Nurturing and love
Eternally in my heart!

Daily I give silent thanks
For the Earth's beaches ~
May we learn to tend them
Clean and unpolluted
Forever beautiful
For generations to come!

Julie Maya

Peace Be With Thee

The sea has such charm, all of its own
When it's peaceful and quiet, morning sunshine, on slow little
wavelets
Shines and twinkles, then even music is heard
I have heard it murmuring, specially in the moonlight
It takes my breath away, it all looks so wonderful
But, it too can be can enemy, when storms and high seas
Ten foot waves can kill, then there is no joy
Men can see no fun, as the sea bursts like guns, over the side of crafts
It can be mighty and strong, but, I can only see at this moment
The peace that it can bring, when the moon is high, and the sea is
soft
Or in the morning, when clouds are pink, then the sea just whispers
Peace be with thee.

Winifred Parkinson

Back To Nature

A little bit of heaven can be yours and yours alone
Just take the time to cultivate a corner of your own
Invite the birds and bees to join you, let them know you care
And you will be rewarded with their company to share

Sit amongst the flowers, watch the caterpillar crawl
Smell the sweetness of the earth, and savour the birds' call
Watch the birds around the table ~ feed your feathered friends
Give them all a sheltered home on which they can depend

The concrete shrouds that men have built to house the human heart
Should be torn down releasing men to make a brand new start
Go back to basics, toil the earth, become at one with nature
Re-invent what man has lost, and give him back his stature

Avril Ann Weryk

The Good Earth

Perhaps the concrete jungle helps us live with ease.
But where would we be without our wonderful trees.
Each spring they astound us with beautiful green leaves.
They help protect us when the hot sun doesn't please.
Yet countless trees are destroyed for greed, this must cease.
Save the good earth!

How sad it would be if we ruin the future.
Of the unborn children of whom we should nurture.
Let all the trees and the parks become a fixture.
To look after and cherish and make a picture.
Our good health and happiness we get from nature.
From the good earth!

It's truly an amazing sight to see seeds grow.
From practically nothing to a lovely show.
To delight all viewers who are not in the know.
Just let them learn the easy system to follow
So they can see their own flowers grow tomorrow.
In the good earth!

Phyllis Dartnell

Leave-Taking

Car packed, maps at the ready,
Fond farewells exchanged;
A last look at the autumnal borders,
Then to reception with the key,
And along the track to the shop
For a parting word: A look in either direction.
Then on to the open road, and away.

Malcolm Cooper

Everything

Everything is for a 'purpose',
No 'matter' how we 'try'
Whatever happens 'day by day'
We have to 'face' to 'get by'

'Anything' can 'happen'
'Anytime' ~ 'Anywhere'
We can't 'stop' it 'happening'
'Can we'
So 'why care'

The 'day' turns into 'night'
The 'darkness' into 'light'
The 'dawn' comes up 'slow'
The 'nights' how 'quick' they go

It's all for a 'purpose'
The 'way' the 'world' goes round
And 'even' if we 'miss the boat'
Our 'feet' are 'on the ground'

E B Holcombe

My Fairy

Today I saw a fairy out in the sky
I went out and she'd gone with no goodbye
I was cross at the fairy for going away
And hoped I could see her another day

The next day I saw a fairy out in the sky
I went out and felt her fly right by
I was cross at the fairy for going away
And hoped I could see her another day

The next day I saw a fairy out in the sky
I tiptoed out to see her and there she lie
She'd fallen into a bramble bush in a state
I went over to help her but it was too late

The fairy disappeared did she die?
Where was my fairy I'd seen in the sky?
I glimpsed through the window it was great
There was the fairy saying, 'Sorry I'm late.'

That day when I saw the fairy out in the sky
She waved in at the window and said, 'Let's fly.'
I flew to my fairy and kissed her soft cheek
We love to go flying at least twice a week.

Amanda Buttress

Victim

A noise in my home late at night,
A stranger should I confront him or take flight?
Maybe I wouldn't get hurt but then again I might.
If I could get outside would anyone take notice of my plight?

Logic told me with the intruder I wasn't strong enough to fight,
The damage and loss was only slight,
I survived and luckily I'm alright,
I won't be sleeping soundly in my bed tonight.

Ann Woolven

Send Love

You really are my everything,
Sweet, serene, just like a dove.
You have made, my life worth living.
When you're away, just send me love.

You're everything, you make my life worthwhile.
Your beauty, like the stars above.
I always long, to see your smile.
When you're away, just send me love.

I'd give you the world, if it were mine,
Sun and moon, and stars above.
You're everything, you are divine,
So when you're away, just send me love.

Jeff Hobson

Season's Dawn

Down below life started to stir,
Mr Earthworm threaded his way.
Come along Scilla and Snowdrop, he said,
There's work for you today.
Snowdrop raised her arms, Scilla stretched her neck,
As they prepared for this year's season,
Follow me, Mr Earthworm said,
I'll make a path for you.
Snowdrop moved her pale white stem
As she followed Earthworm's path,
Come along Scilla, Snowdrop said,
We must hurry to reach the dawn,
Scilla raised her arms to protect her delicate head,
I'm coming she said, as she followed Snowdrop's path.
It will be good to see the light.
Be careful Mr Earthworm said,
The snow's begun to melt,
There'll just be time to greet the dawn,
Before good people rise this morn,
Snowdrop's stem had changed to green,
her bell-like head to nod,
As she greeted this season's dawn,
Scilla thrust her arms into the light,
To join her friends in this wonderful sight.
Scilla's blue head and Snowdrop's white bell,
Brought the promise of Spring
From Winter's knell.

Ada Brookes Reid

Untitled

In this mysterious array of interesting displays
Of statues and plants and ponds with no names
Distant thoughts pass like the burr of a plane
Not leaving nor landing suspended by time

And by a tree resting in perfect peace
In this garden of far off conjured ease
I saw life slipping from its exactness
And the whole world seemed valuable and relaxing.

Michael James Fuller

My Wants
(After a hard day teaching)

I want to be wild, I want to be straight.
I want to love, I want to hate.
I want to be busy, I want to be lazy.
I want to be bright, I want to be dozey.
I want to be serious, I want to be silly.
I want to be proper, I want to be dizzy.

I want to be shy, I want to be out.
I want to scream, I want to shout.
I want to be with someone, I want to be alone.
I want to be jolly, I want to moan.
I want to indulge, I want to be healthy.
I want to be poor, I want to be wealthy.

I want not to care, I want to be 'green'.
I want to be invisible, I want to be seen.
I want to be young, I want to be old.
I want to be quiet, I want to be bold.
I want to be happy, I want to be sad.
I want to be good, I want to be bad.

I want to be simple, I want to be deep.
I want to laugh, I want to weep.
I want to write, I want to be creating.
I want to be private, I want to be sharing.
I want to be drunk, I want to be sober.
I want to be alive, I want it all over.

You see ~
I just want to be me!

Julia Trevarthen

Our King Of Hearts

If you had only stayed strong, when the game seemed so long
For your tunnel showed light and was not endless.
You were winning each day, and the trumps that you played
Made you very well liked ~ and not friendless.

There were times when you'd rush; put forward a flush
Instead of waiting a while.
And though good at the game, you were never to blame
When others played out with their prile.

There were times when you 'twisted' and occasionally went 'bust',
And if only you'd said with each deal,
'No card in this pack is 'gonna' put me off track.'
You would still have control of the wheel.

But 'twas that final 'Ace Card' (which you found so hard)
We wished you'd stopped to think over and rest.
For there was no need to stand, to prove your good hand,
We knew you'd a 'Heart of the best'.

Now sadly you've gone, but the game still goes on
And each day when the deal starts
From beginning to end, we think of you 'friend'.
Yes 'Andy', You're 'Our King of Hearts.'

Today and everyday ~ John and Ray

John Watkins

Construction

We live in an age of confusion
When subjects no longer are known,
And achievements are just a delusion
People think they can work on their own!

They scan many exam papers
To find questions the same every time.
Then memorise those which are favoured
And pass thinking they are sublime.

The proudly display their diplomas
An example being AMI Struct E
To boast is really a misnomer
As these days it's quite plain to see.

Modern design is a credit
To display the style of today,
But to ignore facts is no merit
When catastrophe comes their way.

So to those engineers of construction,
Past manuals are there for your use.
Many works over centuries have proven
You cannot such knowledge abuse.

D R Thomas

Motorways Or Countryways

You speed along the motorway
As fast, as fast can be
Hardly noticing the scenery
As you rush from A to B

Sometimes in traffic, sometimes alone
The miles just race away
It's incredible the distance
You can travel in a day

Sometimes you meet a traffic jam
And then you crawl along
Avoiding all the traffic cones
As you join the busy throng

Until at last you filter through
And you quickly travel on
Striving to regain some time
You imagine is lost and gone

Then by contrast I travelled
Along the country ways
On a motorcycle I journeyed
On many a happy day

With plenty of time to gaze
And really see such views
Fields, woods and flowers
Countless colours and hues

Remote villages and places
I came across by chance
Some too small to mention
But more worthy than a glance

Who knows what's around the corner?
Who knows what is in store?
Every place has something of interest
Every place, a place of lore

Terry Daley

Celebrity City Supporter
(In praise of Phil Coulter)

Page remains blank
as I try to magic profound visions
from a stubborn sleeve ~
images to encapsulate
Phil's contribution.

Manual crank
to 'vocabulary-gland' transmission;
water through a sieve,
worthy words precipitate
through my confusion.

Then it comes, thank
God ~ insight, conceptual incision!
Simply I but leave
his own works to adulate
this institution.

Perry McDaid

Hello? Anyone There?

I sit awhile beneath the bough of an overhang
And the genesis of the earth
Reaches for my thoughts.
Soil and womb, soil and tomb,
Become one in time.
Ancient and modern all is the same,
Begat and begot, begin and forgot,
What is time but a tick and a tock
Of a modern day clock?
Hello and goodbye, the earth and the sky
Opposites merge to infinity's surge.
Light breaks at the dawn of the coffee pot morn,
Light fades in the night on the mating delight.
Woman and man bear the seed of unborn,
We are ourselves part genesis spawn.
These things I know, answers I know not,
The mystique still enthrals,
Hells! Heavens! And Camelots!
I remain seated beneath the bough,
Of an overhang, and ponder and wonder,
And ponder and wonder . . . Hello? Anyone there?

Elwyn Johnson

Man's Best Friend

Black as the night was my faithful friend,
Her nose bore a small speck of white,
She welcomed me home, at the day's end,
With a bark and never a bite.

How unfair it seems, a dog's life span
When compared to that of a man.
Our hearts they steal, then bitter blow,
Their course is run, they have to go.

But we are the richer; although bereft:
We still see them there, though long they've left.
We'll never forget them, true to the end,
A dog's not for always, but still man's best friend.

Roger Caswell

Cottage Window

Darkness falls and down the street
lights come on like houses' eyes
When peeping in through open curtains
a cosy scene before us lies

A roaring fire with logs piled high
mantle clock and cosy chair
Peace and quiet beckons to us
safe from all our woe and care

A book discarded halfway open
homely ornaments in their place
Slippers waiting by the fireside
secure relaxing cosy space

Someone enters to the scene
with cup in hand and settles down
Quiet tranquillity glanced when passing
walking on without a sound

Lynda Tegg

A Treasured Heritage

The garden reflected a flower show,
    Beautiful blooms, even I didn't know.
A sea of Poppies of every hue,
    Shed ripened seed for blooms anew.
A bed of Red Roses with scent so sweet,
    Had with baby's breath sown in between.
Giant tall Pom-Poms clover pink,
    Sip from a fountain spray to drink.
Carpets of Lavender, so sweetly scented,
    Where Bees sipped pollen and droned contented.
Massed flower beds stretched beside green velvet lawns,
    Reached a Mansion built with grace and form.
Imagine living here in ages past,
    With true love given with joy that lasts.
Making History throughout the ages,
    Recorded and read in Historic pages.
Always the splendour of nature, bringing quality to life,
    A treasured corner of England without war or strife!

Margaret Hubball

the dreamer

the dreamer from her slumber woke
wiped the last remnants of imagination from her mind
out in the world she must conform to what they say
original thoughts are forbidden
through the day there is only black and white
no colours to broaden her mind
but when night falls and she is on her own
blissful slumber returns once more
in her dreams the colours of a life once known
of a childhood now forgotten come flooding back
in a torrent as vigorous as the cascading falls of niagara
imagination can run wild in the dream
days of happy laughter running free as the ocean
then she was her true self
not having to conform to society's wishes
don't dream of tomorrow
the uneventful tomorrow
yesterday is where the future lies

Rebecca Hebson

Choices

Life is a Gift beyond understanding
Yet humanity enfolds simple gems.
A myriad of emotions speak in vibrant tones
~ and the choice is ever ours.

A World Umbrella of care and love shines through
Giving immeasurable joy and peace
As down the centuries
Human endeavour and fulfilment are pursued.

Life is a Road into creativity
Hard dedication humouring every path.
So unique with challenges swift to beckon us
~ and the choice is ever ours.

Such harsh injustice and schemes of ill are wrought
Tossing excruciating hate and pain
To fuel grim miseries,
People respond with resilience and courage.

Life is a Torch shining unconditionally
Where harmonious ripples quietly stir
And shadows so heavy fade in silent trance
~ and the choice is ever ours.

A large arena with pain and hurt cries out
Leaving insufferable fear and woe
Yet the very simplicity in existing
Defies misery as miracles do occur.

Life is a Trip within panoramas.
Strong prejudices abounding sadly harsh,
A torrent of torment shouts with horrid force
~ and the choice is ever ours.

A strong awareness of heart and soul walks in
Bringing uncompromising faith and hope
To soften those nightmares
Often tremendous and unnerving hills climbed.

Life is a Door opening unexpectedly
And responses reveal happy chance
With dawning light crystal clear for seeing eyes
~ and the choice is ever ours.

Margaret Ann Wheatley

Auld Lang Syne

People gather in Trafalgar Square at this time each year,
Waiting for Big Ben to proclaim that a New Year is here.
Dancing and singing is the name of the game,
A drunk and disorderly New Year's Eve, nothing's changed.

Crowds of revellers gather on this special night,
But I regret there will probably be a fight.
That's life, and over the years it's been the same,
These people should hang their heads in shame.

There is a great feeling to be had from this day,
Knowing life still goes on, sometimes without affray.
This is not just another New Year for us to take,
It is the start of a New Millennium for us to make.

Roy Coppin

The Tattooed Man

I sat in the park ~ watching the children at play,
hearing their laughter ~ while they were being chased.
A big bald-headed man, like a kid himself,
scooping them in his arms ~ and putting them down.

He came and sat beside me, wiping his face,
I noticed his tattoos, covering his arms, and neck.
I wondered how could anyone do this to themselves?
Maybe on the dole, takes drugs ~ a 'misplace'.

He muttered in his deep voice, 'They sure are a handful.'
I asked if they were his ~ he turned and looked at me.
Grey eyes smiling, ' No, love, they're orphans ~ no folks
of their own ~ just a day out ~ to call their own.'

He told me, he was a volunteer ~ with three others,
working for an overseas Aid Charity.
These young kids had lost their own ~ due to war.
He said, he was once an orphan ~ and knew the score.

I held out my hand ~ and he gently held mine,
We sat, side by side, he and I.
I felt so bad ~ to misjudge this big, tattooed man,
I felt so humble ~ and privileged, to know this kind man.

Diana Beck-Martin

My Little Treasure
(Dedicated to my Granddaughter Caitlin Beth)

Oh how I love to see your smiles
And how your energy goes on for miles
Your little face, hands and feet
Are all so perfect and so very sweet.

To see such expressions and big toothy grin
I even love your double chins, your chubby legs,
Your soft silk skin
Oh I'm so glad you're not thin.

I feel so proud of my granddaughter
Even when she's very naughty
You just smile, I just melt
How can I be cross with you for long
When I'd really like to sing you a song.

To make you smile, to make you laugh
Whether or not I look daft
Crawling on the floor, hanging on a door
Even when I'm very sore.

But you're worth it because I get so
Much pleasure,
From being your Grandma,
You're my little treasure.

Maggie Whitfield

June Night

Under a toadstool
Quite out of sight
Sat a wee elf
On a moonlight night.

The stars shone bright
And a nightingale trilled
And the air with the scent
Of flowers was filled.

So he sat and thought
Of the stars and moon
Of the wind in the trees
But all too soon
A cock crowed loud
And the night was gone
So off he flew
On the wings of song.

Sylvia Bryan

Tender Touch

Darling, look into my eyes . . .
The love you see wears no disguise.
All I have got I'll share with you.
Am I reaching you?
Darling, I wish I knew.

Darling, can you feel the urge?
The love inside me seems to surge.
Sweetheart, am I breaking through?
I am so in love with you.
Yes, so in love it's true.

So . . .
Love me, darling,
Because I need your
Love so much.
Hold me, darling,
Because I love your
Tender touch.

Darling, if you are all alone . . .
Just call me on the telephone.
I will come and comfort you.
Holding on to you.
Making love to you.

Darling, if your heart is in pain,
I will cheer you up again.
The love will never fade away.
No, never fade away.
Never go astray.

So . . .
Love me, darling,
Because I need your
Love so much.
Hold me, darling,
Because I love your
Tender touch.

Peter Steele

Our Cornish Mines

Familiar buildings fall away,
Crumble slowly, day by day.
Noticed not by passers-by,
Missed by the sharpest eye.

People visit, people sit.
Yet these people never notice it.
Young Johnny plays here with his mate,
At these places left, to disintegrate.

No valid cause or impediment,
They knock one down with full consent!
Ghosts of workmen watch helplessly,
Nowhere now, to brew their tea.

Is it too late to try persuading?
~ Our heritage is quickly fading.
Let's build them up, let's have respect
For our Cornish mines, which they neglect.

Though listed, the ignorance of man
Destroy the stacks because they can!
These mines, they fed us through the years ~
Did they *have* to prove our fears?

Must stop this mindless, sad destruction
And plan instead, some reconstruction.

Jean M Tonkin

Spring

At least somebody wants to see the sky,
At least somebody wants to see the sun.
To see the little birds fly,
And to see the little buds come.

To see the lambs a-gambolling,
Beneath the billowing cloud,
To see the snowdrops blooming,
And forgetting that thunder loud.

Nevenka Kojic

An October Boating Lake

Saddening water. Battleship grey skies
although no battles are raging. No thunder or lightning
slice through the leaden. Wandering the edges. Adrift
in melancholia.

You have stolen my language. My phrases shattered.
My cadences smothered by torpor. It is never my acknowledged
that I walk around my parameters. It is not my world ~ seen Muse
that I laud and carefully smoke my test for.

Who but you could carefully knife along the words
and lay open the pulsing within?
Who else would rejoice in induced suppuration?

Now I vomit up gobbets of fractured bile.
Dissonance and inarticulacy are the keys.
How can I change anything? Distraught, I throw my thoughts
wildly, into the cold of the lake.

Ade Macrow

A Warm Welcome

Everyone's pleased to be near me when it's cold and frosty outside
When moonbeams shine on ice crystals making them sparkle with
pride
And breath spills away from chilled nostrils like dragons being
vilified
As footsteps tread on the hard frozen ground ringing out each
nearing stride

Warmth from me radiates rapidly attracting people like moths in the
night
As my hot fiery furnace burns fiercely almost totally hidden from
sight
Smoke from my log burning stove rises up to a goodly height
Sending smoke signals into the night sky high above my oasis bright

Hands are rubbed briskly together all seeking renewed feelings and
life
Chilled by the icy cold weather bringing chaos trouble and strife
Sensations return to numb fingers as if being slashed by a knife
As owners come in and meet up with friends away from where frost
is rife

Pleasantries are exchanged and chairs are brought to my side
As the regulars chat about the harsh winter chill from which they all
try to hide
My heat brings welcome relief as they joke about nature defied
As they feed fresh logs through my open top watching sparks ride up
and collide

Idle chatter comes to an end as they finish their drinks and go home
Quitting my warming presence no longer chilled to the bone
Drained glasses are stacked on the tables and I'm left to myself alone
As they wend their way from the country pub where my welcoming
warmth is well known

Keith B Osborne

My Life

I was born in August, 1954
In a hospital built in memory of the war.
Today it just does not exist at all.
It's now a block of flats and a brick wall.

At school, I'd pass exams, but fail some too.
Sometimes I'd feel so happy, others blue.
I'd go to Bispham College and they'd say,
'Well done, you've passed A-Level Law today!'

When unemployed, it really got me down.
I'd feel badly rejected, and I'd frown.
My railway book at York really did help
To make me smile and feel pleased with myself.

Sometimes I'm blue, but much more often glad.
For the good times by far outweigh the bad!

A Marlow

All Changed

Quiet now is the house where once we as children did sing.
All is quiet in the house where once there was an awful din.
We all have left the family house, where we shared so much joy.
Quiet is the house but memories still linger of when I was a boy.
Now no children run up the stairs, or slam the kitchen door.
Now no children race in for tea, at the hour of four.
It is now a guest house, a B and B they say.
But it looked so shabby, as I passed the other day.

Don Goodwin

Imagine

Imagine that you
Could see into the future
What it has in store for you
Imagine that the oceans
Were grey instead of blue
Imagine that the birds
No longer sing their songs
Imagine that all the trees
Have all long since gone
Imagine all the meadows
Lifeless silent and bare
Imagine all of this
Yet no one seems to care

Greeny

A Smile From The Heart

How could I forget
The day you were born
The sun was just waking
A bold bright new dawn

And yet it seemed only
Perhaps a second before
That a child I had lost
Could I take anymore?

My world had just ended
My smile had been taken
No bright new dawn
No sun to awaken.

But I look at you now
As years have passed by
With your blond curly hair
And that glint in your eye.

The joy that you give
Makes me smile every day
A reason to live
A reason to say

That I'll treasure your love
All my life through
And I'll always be smiling
Just because you are you.

H Middleton

What's In A Smile?

The wishful smile on my mother's face
Remembering days long gone.
On that summer day
As she sat 'neath the trees,
She knew she hadn't got long.
The cheeky grin on my grandson's face,
The day he learned to crawl ~
That changed to a startled expression
When, trying to stand,
He started to fall.
The smile of pride on my father's face,
As he walked me down the aisle.
My happiness reflected
On my husband's face
When he gave me that lovely smile.
The look of apprehension
On my children's faces
As they requested a special thing
And when I agreed,
The smiles of relief
Seemed to make my heart sing.
How can I put a value
On what's reflected in a smile?
If you greet each day
With laughter in your eyes,
Then your life will be worthwhile.

Mary Plucinski

Smile Surprise

Bad moods often cloud my day
When the sun forgets to ray
Little things get me upset
Bossy neighbours, heavy debt.

This day differed, made me proud
As a beam diffused the cloud
When my baby son Sam smiled
My heart sang for that small child.

Lineless contours of his face
Crinkled with a happy grace
One brief gesture warmed me through
Helplessly I smiled too.

What had caused the babe to smile?
Tickling him is not my style
When I do he starts to wriggle
Seldom has a decent giggle.

This time he looked to the sky
Watched translucent spirits fly
Thoughts that skittered through his head
Made him laugh 'til he glowed red.

The spirits made me chortle too
As they made my dreams come true
To see my son cloaked in bliss
Is welcome as an angel's kiss.

Gleaming eyes and chubby chin
Rounded face that makes me grin
As he learns his ABC
He can smile along with me.

Nick Smith

Craig

When I first met him on that hot summer's day
He was lying by the pool whilst the other children played.
I knew that he was special from the very first glance
And that I could reach him, if given half the chance.
I chatted about the others who were swimming about
And all the places I'd visited whilst on my day out.
He didn't seem to be listening but I still persevered
With a kind of verbal assault on his small, shell-like ears.
I took hold of his hands and held them in mine
Then planted small kisses, one at a time
One on his forehead then one on his nose
The next on his cheeks that the sun had made glow
The last one on his chin and then I stood back
And that's when I saw he was going to react.
His eyes turned towards me and then it appeared
The most wonderful smile that reduced me to tears.
He wasn't completely locked in his own world
I had somehow managed to get through to this child,
Our holiday lasted for just one more week
But every day, at some point, I'd make sure we'd meet.
He would greet my arrival with a shout of delight
Whilst wildly thrashing his wasted limbs about.
And then when I spoke, it would appear once more,
That million dollar smile that I really adored.
His mother was delighted that he had been able to respond
And during those few days, we developed quite a bond.
Craig was five years old but looked only about two
And doctors had said there was nothing they could do.
He'll never go to school and will not reach his teens
But his smile must be the best this world has ever seen.

Barbara Bramley

The Language Of The Smile

A glance by chance,
The warmest smile.
So simple no reason,
Difficult to describe.

We were strangers,
Two women, who happened to be,
Shopping for food on a grey afternoon,
Sharing a smile that changed my mood.

Sometimes it happens,
We never know where,
A moment of friendship,
Two people can share.

I thought to myself, as
I walked to my car,
The silent language of the smile.
It speaks with movement,

Of the face, and then
Is gone, with so much haste.
The feeling of friendship,
That lifted my soul.

I know it seems foolish,
To judge by a smile,
But I really did feel,
That a friendship

Could seal, on that
Grey afternoon, when
Two strangers met,
And shared a smile,
And a glance,
By chance.

Carol Brierley

My Grandson's First Steps

First the crawl
Then pulling himself up
Look I am standing tall
Standing up drinking from his cup

Cup down I am on the go
He reaches for the next chair
I can do it oh! No
Down he goes I give a cuddle and some care

Then he is off once more
I can see that look
Up he goes holding on his little feet
Going across the floor
Then he turns I hold out my arms
Come on his hand I took

That wonderful smile of pride
It says it all
I can walk not down I fall
I smile a Grandmother joy oh!
How he has tried.

Abbie

Like Father Like Son

A four-year-old sat still in church
to see his baby sister named;
the priest in black and white appeared,
'Oh, here comes God!' the boy exclaimed.

At eight he knew he wasn't God
for God lived high above the sky ~
a man who gazed down on the world,
who saw you with his eagle eye.

At twelve he knew God's not a man
but spirit in earth's outer space:
magnetic force or radio waves,
life forces with a human face.

He, sixteen now, knew a big bang
hurled suns and stars light years away,
with God behind all galaxies.
He turned to Christ for every day.

At twenty-two his M. Sc.
set him designing crafts for space
to fly from earth within his God:
to seek in Mars an alien race.

At twenty-six he pledged his troth
and soon became a family man,
a stalwart at the local church;
to follow Christ and God to scan.

And now he takes his son just four
to see his little sister named;
the boy looks as the priest appears,
'Oh, here comes God,' the boy exclaimed.

Owen Edwards

Smiles

Miles of smiles, from me to you,
Smile with everything you do,
Smile at people on your way,
They'll smile back and make your day.
Tonic better than a pill,
Smiles will never make you ill.

I look in the mirror, I smile at me,
I smile at everyone I see.
Boy or girl, don't bother me,
I like to smile.
Try it and see.

People ask me why I grin,
I say to avoid a double chin.
I smile all day, at work and play,
But will that fat chin go away?

Smile at babies in their pram,
Smile and greet that old gentleman.
He told me once I'd made his day,
He'd made mine, I have to say.
But the smile that melts my heart away,
Is the one from my love,
At the end of each day.

Georgie

The Smile Of The Fire's Flames

Watching, staring at the fire's flames
as they dance and dance the time away.
They seem to smile; row upon row
lifting my spirits with their glow.

Miserable soul, downcast and feeling low
awaken from this trance.
Life offers more, so do not abort,
their smile is for me perchance.

See in yonder flames
the peace, the calm that tames.
Their warmth and comfort
speaks volumes to the inner man.

Cast aside that frown they say
in their own silent way.
Cheer up is their beckoning call
making me feel ten feet tall.

J Henderson Lightbody

Tricks Of The Mind

What kind of evil sickness
    steals away the mind?
'till there's just a shrunken shadow
    of a woman left behind.
What kind of awful torment
    leaves me struggling to recall
The one who loved and cared,
    when there's no trace of her at all?
She cannot speak, she cannot walk,
    she does not know me now,
But still I bend to kiss her and caress
    the shrivelled brow.
Suddenly she's smiling, laughter in her
    eye
Memories of childhood, of all the years
    gone by.
It lasted just a moment, some short
    circuit in the brain
That made her know and love me,
    her daughter once again.
So when this dementia's over
    and all her struggles cease,
When the torture is all ended,
    and at last she finds her peace,
Let me forget the horror
    By some trick my mind beguile
To keep with me forever,
    My beloved Mother's smile.

Sue Boden

Smiles

It may begin to curl and crack
in answer to a swift attack.
Starting in the corner with a flicker,
small but growing infectious snicker.
Spreading quickly, taking up slack,
reaching the point, no going back,
express train, on well-worn track,
from city gent to urban slicker,
Smile.

Tearful, on a different tack,
joy supplies the winning knack.
Destiny can declare a sticker
banishing blame, bogy, bicker.
Myriads make up the pack.
Smile.

Ken G Watson

Smiles From Heaven

It's been a long time since I've seen you
How I've yearned to see your smile
Shared the laughter in your eyes
And sat and talked with you a while

Our children now feel better
The way that children always do
I see the way they're growing
And my thoughts return to you

Their laughter is your echo
Their faces smile at me
And then I know for certain
It's your smile that I can see

It's been a long time since I've seen you
But you'll always be a part
Of the children that we made
Their smiles will ease my broken heart

Christine Crook

Totally Nuts

A smile always seems to dance upon her lips,
Then, without warning
The laughter as if held in
Bursts forth and spills uncontrollably around
Thus, sending little smiles onto onlooker's lips.

She's always happy,
A bit bossy
Definitely eccentric
Bold and bubbly,
Fab, fun and feisty,
Totally nuts
She's Joyce.

Lesley-Ann Curdy

The Smile

It appears to the patient
Such a lot of fuss
As each little detail
Is checked by nurse
No false teeth, no hearing aid
As into oblivion she does fade
Off on the trolley
For the dreaded op
Would rather be going
For a trip to the shop
But alas it's a day
At the theatre for me
'Cause I've trouble
In the nether region you see
But I'll know for sure
It's been all worthwhile
When I awake to see
That sweet nurse *smile*

Janie Chafer

An Ode To Marriage

First choose, then hear thee's desire,
Dwell truth to avoid illusion,
Choose love that your love aspire,
Sing a song for the perfection.

With that it's thee's sweet desire,
Let thee show how much thee loves kiss,
Then light starry spirit of peace,
It thee for'ver that aspire.

Be proud and glow like a rose,
Thee's heart will be aye to you close,
Such a thought will both of you bind;
So, keep love feelings: just and kind.

Love each other and faithfully,
Going 'n' Coming will the same be,
Let innocence within both shine,
That way both will aged so divine.

Oh, how sweet and fair life will be,
Glow with that, which nourishes thee,
Leave profound living memory,
Pass living record t' Family.

Milan Trubarac

Summer's End

The glossy sheen has worn from vibrant petals ~
deep colour fades, bled by an ardent sun ~
and brittle leaves curl, tired with disillusion,
grown listless as the swallows to be gone.

Horizons ache, the hollow sky dreams distance;
his smile is empty ~ the frail ghost of love
haunts the evening, whispers in far forests,
her skin is cool, the silence hangs above

their melancholy, shared but all unuttered,
the sharpened breeze blows callous and unkind,
the hillside blurs with shadows and the roses
sigh like lovers ~ wistful but resigned.

Dark lashes veil the measure of nostalgia ~
her clear-eyed blue transmutes to sombre grey ~
they watch the daylight drain from fields together
and feel their summer slowly slip away.

Jean M Harvey

That Inward Eye

Out of the distance their faces swim,
    Out of the mists of time,
Kindly regarding each childish whim,
    Showing us heights to climb.

Helper and teacher, aunt and friend,
    From babyhood I recall
How each some special gift would spend,
    But my parents over all.

My mother's black hair and deep blue eyes,
    Her gentle but lively wit;
Tales of her childhood she often told,
    A drama she'd make of it.

My father had bright blue Saxon eyes,
    From central England's plain,
Musical, skilled in many crafts ~
    How seldom a cross word came!

At thirteen, I was near to death,
    Six weeks in bed I lay ~
It's thanks to Mother's ceaseless care
    That I am here today.

One night, I opened conscious eyes
    And there my parents stood,
Leaning upon the brass-railed bed,
    Together, come what would.

'Why is Mother crying?' I thought,
    So I the corner turned,
I saw my father's steadfast look
    As I to life returned.

I see them still with inward eye:
So I may find them when I die.

    Kathleen M Hatton

Briefest Love

She looked at me for one brief moment I was in love
She passed by and in that passing I heard songs above
Informing me that Cupid had struck his arrow correct
I had to find where she went as my heart became vexed
I searched and made enquiries many thought of me as mad
I gave a perfect description the only thing I had
Seeing her reflected in a shop windowpane
'Twas a glancing moment she was causing me such pain
Alas thought I when day was done and in a saddened mood
Wandering as I travelled home upon this beauty I did brood
I thought I felt a strange caress as I prepared to retire
This satisfied my inner thoughts this was my lovely desire

Whilst waiting for transport in the pouring rain
I saw her gazing up at me with love she could not sustain
She then reached forward to my welcoming open arms
And in that torrential downpour of that vision I held her charms
Many witnessed my actions they became alarmed
And eventually the police were called I was detained by their strong
arms
Causing an affray in a public place I was sentenced and warned
Called an utter disgrace all because of you and your beautiful face
she now comes to me often with those lovely eyes making my life
Complete she of me never denies
I thought I was in love now she has been spirited away
Never speaking as those eyes told me all she had to say

R D Hiscoke

126

Of My Father

I see a picture of my father
Amongst the other men
How I wish I had known them
In the black and white year of then 1921.

I see a picture of my father
Standing with a horse so big
Then read about the weeks work they had before them
Were they ever sick.

I see a picture of my father
Shortly before the second world war
A tractor he had by then
Gone with the miles of walking behind a horse
Yet both were still good friends.

Keith L Powell

True Love!

There are many different kinds of love
Each one a gift from God above
He fills the aching void within our heart
With a balm to heal, and let us start
To live a life of happiness again
With someone to share it, easing the pain we felt before
As now we have someone to love and to adore
Don't ever lose this precious gift
Don't ever let there be a rift
That tears apart two trusting hearts
Two loving souls who should play their part
Together caring for each other
Could be a boy and girl
Or a child and mother
Then sorrow will rear its ugly head
Before you know it ~ love is dead
Oh, how you will pine and rue the day
You threw this beautiful love away
Every moment of every day
You will have to think and humbly pray
That God will hear your plea of despair
And grant your prayer
To give back to you, that precious love
But God is fair, and God is just
He will see if you deserve His trust
Ask His forgiveness once again
He will give back to you, your love again.

Margaret McHugh

The Power House

Chimneys tall
Chimneys small
Chimneys fat and chubby,
Billowing smoke
Clouds all choked,
In power there is money

Chugging boats on water deep
Full to the brim a black heap,
Black gold to feed machine
Choking billowing smoke,
In power there is money

Black gold from down the pit
Chiselled by men some unfit,
Danger lurks deep in the mine,
One of those men could be thine

Coal dust chokes and fills your chest
They can only do their best,
Death came early at this time
No one's healthy down a mine

Many hours are spent below
Deep beneath a town or street,
From every house a loved one works,
Chiselling, digging, for all his worth

Far away a bird he sings,
When he stops, danger brings
In dead of night, a siren, loud,
Fills all hearts with dread.
Quite often when this sound shrills out
A loved one ends up dead.

Caroline Halliday

Listen

Listen and hear ~ listen and learn.
A powerful gift, which takes our time.
The key to problems, needing our help,
Yet a blessing for those with mountains to climb.

Too many complacent, too many don't care.
Dismissive, cocooned in their worlds.
If they could spare a minute, to listen, that's all
To those less fortunate, Lady Luck has spurned.

Make life more bearable,
And help share the load.
Reap rewards without measure,
As we all travel the same road.

Gwyneth Cleworth

A Seaside Fortune Teller

Cross my palm with silver
And your fortune I will tell
And I see here in my crystal ball
There's times you've not been well

For I see you've had a hard life
And worries through the years
And although there has been laughter
There has also been some tears

But all that is now changing
And a journey I can see
To a far exotic island
Or just Southend-on-Sea

And there's some money coming
Do you do the pools my dear
For it says so in my crystal ball
And it shows it very clear

I can see the letters M and R
and the initials APQ
It could be distant cousins
Or someone close to you

I can also see a stranger
He's tall and lives quite near
And he'll be knocking on your door
You mark my words my dear

And you'll also have a long life
With many years of ease
For you and for your loved one
And that's three quid, if you please

R H Turke

Home From New Zealand

Home again, with memories and pictures;
    Sunshine, warm seas and soft winds
    Now far way.

Home again, Westbourne, the village church,
    And Easter, shining through the English rain
    On an April day.

Home again, I listen to your voices
    Recorded here for ever, just for me
    When I'm alone.

Home again, I still see Mount Rangitoto
    Far away, beyond the distant sea
    On the blue horizon.

M M Mose

Pigeon Lane

A cloudless sky
The warm sun glistens on the water
Yet still a cold wind blows
Trees rough bushes rustle their leaves
Water runs freely
Rushing
Dabble and splash
Seagulls call
Scavenge for food
Through leftover rubbish
Not one shopping trolley
But three
Original stone bridges
Over the stream
A wooden seat
To take in a moment.

Angela Couzens

In Transit

Slowly drifting,
Desperately seeking,
Something to hold on to,
To call his own.

Packing his case,
And he's leaving.
He's got to keep moving,
Once again deserting.

He feels he's been pushed,
Outcast from the norm.
Rumours are to be hushed,
Won't wait to be scorned.

Tales of the unacceptable,
Feelings of the unsociable.
Those who are intolerant
Now weep their loss.

Karen Gaynord

I've Lost My Pet

He sits alone at dead of night
His form translucent pearly white,
I say his name and call him 'dear'
He still remains tho' I go near,
He turns his head to look at me
But then I know he cannot see,
I stoop with hands outstretched to touch
The little form I loved so much,
My hands hold nothing as they meet
Oh, memories are bitter sweet . . .
The hurt is still there and I cry
I know he's gone and I must try,
To live without him, to the end
My 'darlin' 'bestest' little friend.

J G Tryhorn

Grandma's Teeth

Grandma's teeth come out every night,
She keeps them in a glass beside the bedside light.
Grandma says they like the exercise,
But I think even Grandma lies!

I've sat and watched them motionless inside the glass,
It's quite a boring way to let the hours pass.
The only movement that I've detected,
Are lots of bubbles being resurrected.

At times Grandma looks rather strange,
Without her teeth her features rearrange.
That once full mouth of pearly whites
Resembles stairs without the flights.

Even Granddad refrains from kissing,
Grandma's lips when teeth are missing.
But I love Grandma just the same,
She's still as sweet and quite insane!

It's such a shame her teeth she neglected,
This causes me some introspection.
What I've learnt to my surprise,
I don't want my teeth taking exercise!

Kim Senior

Television

Today's
Entertainment industry
Lights up the
Enjoyment of people.
Visions people have seen
Images, like computer graphics,
Seeing not believing.
Inventions making television more interesting by
Overriding people's imagination.
No-one knows how far we can go with *television*.

Philip Kilgour

The Philosophical Drinker

He sits in a corner all by himself
One of life's philosophical thinkers
A half pint in hand, a practised stealth
Surveys the other drinkers
His aim for today as always
Is to keep watch on the bar
In hope that he might spot the mug
To purchase him a jar
He sidles to his victim
A smile, a nudge, a wink
And in bold anticipation
He finishes his drink
He strikes up conversation
On current affairs, he's a star
Then asked if he'd like another
He says, 'Oh nice one, ta.'
The philosophical drinker
Is there till closing time
And philosophically speaking
He hasn't spent a dime.

Lynne Marie White